W9-CDH-480

A LITTLE BOOK
OF ALCOHOL

by the same author

Games and Activities for Exploring Feelings
Giving Children the Confidence to Navigate Emotions and Friendships
ISBN 978 1 84905 222 1
eISBN 978 0 85700 459 8

101 Things to Do on the Street
Games and Resources for Detached, Outreach and Street-Based Youth Work
2nd edition
ISBN 978 1 84905 187 3
eISBN 978 0 85700 419 2

Let's Talk Relationships
Activities for Exploring Love, Sex, Friendship and Family with Young People
2nd edition
ISBN 978 1 84905 136 1
eISBN 978 0 85700 340 9

Cyberbullying
Activities to Help Children and Teens to Stay Safe in a Texting, Twittering, Social Networking World
ISBN 978 1 84905 105 7
eISBN 978 0 85700 228 0

Working with Young Men
Activities for Exploring Personal, Social and Emotional Issues
2nd edition
ISBN 978 1 84905 101 9
eISBN 978 0 85700 282 2

Working with Young Women
Activities for Exploring Personal, Social and Emotional Issues
2nd edition
ISBN 978 1 84905 095 1
eISBN 978 0 85700 372 0

A LITTLE BOOK OF ALCOHOL

ACTIVITIES TO EXPLORE ALCOHOL ISSUES WITH YOUNG PEOPLE

Second Edition

Vanessa Rogers

Jessica Kingsley *Publishers*
London and Philadelphia

First published in 2006 by the National Youth Agency
Second edition published in 2012
by Jessica Kingsley Publishers
73 Collier Street,
London N1 9BE, UK
and
400 Market Street, Suite 400
Philadelphia, PA 19106, USA

www.jkp.com

Copyright © Vanessa Rogers 2012

All rights reserved. No part of this publication may be reproduced in any material form (including photocopying of any pages other than those marked with a ✓, storing it in any medium by electronic means and whether or not transiently or incidentally to some other use of this publication) without the written permission of the copyright owner except in accordance with the provisions of the Copyright, Designs and Patents Act 1988 or under the terms of a licence issued by the Copyright Licensing Agency Ltd, Saffron House, 6–10 Kirby Street, London EC1N 8TS. Applications for the copyright owner's written permission to reproduce any part of this publication should be addressed to the publisher.

Warning: The doing of an unauthorised act in relation to a copyright work may result in both a civil claim for damages and criminal prosecution.

All pages marked ✓ may be photocopied for personal use with this programme, but may not be reproduced for any other purposes without the permission of the publisher.

Library of Congress Cataloging in Publication Data
A CIP catalog record for this book is available from the Library of Congress

British Library Cataloguing in Publication Data
A CIP catalogue record for this book is available from the British Library

ISBN 978 1 84905 303 7
eISBN 978 0 85700 628 8

Printed and bound in Great Britain by Bell and Bain Ltd, Glasgow

CONTENTS

ACKNOWLEDGEMENTS

I would like to thank:

Dave Price (A-DASH), Donna Lancaster (Youth Worker), Hertfordshire Youth Connexions, Gillian Porter (QE11), Deborah Mulroney (HCC School Improvement and Development Service), Joshua Oakes-Rogers (Simon Balle School), Darren Godfrey (Essex Youth Service), Geoff Fisher (Peterborough Youth Service) and Ann McKay (Youth Worker).

Thanks also to any other youth workers who have been a part of the projects mentioned.

ABOUT THE AUTHOR

Vanessa Rogers is a qualified teacher and youth worker with a master's degree in Community Education. She has over ten years' experience within the Hertfordshire Youth Service both at practitioner and management levels. Prior to achieving national recognition for her work Vanessa managed a wide range of services for young people, including a large youth centre and targeted detached projects for Hertfordshire County Council. She now devises and delivers professional development training and writes for *Youth Work Now*. In addition she has been commissioned to devise training packs for a wide range of organizations, including the BBC.

This book is one of 20 practical resources written by Vanessa to support the development of creative youth work and social education.

Her website www.vanessarogers.co.uk gives detailed information about further titles, training and consultancy visits.

INTRODUCTION

Deciding whether to drink, or not, is a personal decision that most people will make at some point when growing up. This resource is a diverse collection of activities developed to help inform that decision. Aimed at those working with young people aged 13–19 (up to 24 with additional needs) in both formal and informal education settings, the activities and games give information, explore values and help build skills, promoting healthy choices.

During their teenage years most young people will come into contact with alcohol at some point. In fact many may have already experimented with drinking long before they reach the legal drinking age. This is not a new phenomenon – people have been drinking and experimenting with alcohol for many thousands of years.

As part of the research for this book I asked adults to take part in a quick survey on Facebook and Twitter. The average age of first time drinking for those who responded in the UK was 13 years old; those in the USA tended to be slightly older, with the average being 15. Interestingly, the same survey revealed that the majority of people were introduced to alcohol by a parent or close family relative, often at a family celebration. This parental induction to alcohol mirrors my professional findings with young people, many of whom told me that their parents buy alcohol for them, for example to take to a party. In short, of those teenagers who drink alcohol under-age, it is often with their parents' blessing.

So this book does not approach the subject with a view to ensuring total abstinence (although temperance is a valid choice for anyone) or set out to demonize alcohol, but rather it contains ideas for ways to encourage young people to talk openly and honestly about the choices they are making and gives them the facts in a non-judgemental way. It is hoped that by exploring the physical, emotional and social impact that alcohol can have on an individual they will make an informed decision to keep safe and healthy into adulthood. And, if they do choose to drink alcohol, it will be responsibly and with respect for both themselves and others.

The book is divided into three sections: Warm-ups, Activities and Review Tips. Each session plan can be used as a 'stand-alone' activity or put together with others to build a comprehensive curriculum over a few weeks.

Warm-ups

This section offers short activities and exercises to open a session around alcohol or to re-energize a group after a discussion. Easy to use, these are ideas to introduce issues and enable you to begin to assess the level of knowledge and attitudes to alcohol within the group.

Activities

Including ideas for group and individual work, these activities look at three main areas:

- Factual information and education about alcohol issues.

- The exploration of attitudes and values, including peer influence and reducing risk.
- Opportunities created to develop the skills to make healthy choices.

Review Tips

The final pages suggest a few ideas for reviewing and reinforcing learning. It is important to allow time at the end of a session for these as they help evaluate the effectiveness of sessions and inform your needs analysis for further work.

GROUND RULES

Alcohol can be a sensitive issue and it is important to consider that some young people come from families who do not drink at all for religious or lifestyle reasons, whilst others have family members or friends with alcohol-related problems.

To ensure a safe learning environment it is good practice to negotiate ground rules with the young people at the start, outlining confidentiality and the limits to it. Refer back to them as the sessions progress so they provide a familiar framework for working safely and respectfully together.

Make it clear before you start that there is no assumption being made that all of the young people have drunk alcohol. It is likely that their experiences will be as varied as their values and attitudes to drinking, dependent on social, physical and emotional factors, which the ideas in this book help to explore.

Equally, as the issues around alcohol can be extremely sensitive, make sure that confidentiality and the need to respect each others' points of view and experiences are fully considered. One rule that I often put forward for inclusion is that no one should ask or be asked personal questions. The aim of this is not to stifle confidences, but to enable young people to relax safe in the knowledge that embarrassing questions will not be fired at them. It also protects facilitators from any intimate questions that may be levelled at them.

ALCOHOL INFORMATION

When discussing alcohol with young people it is important to remember that not everyone chooses to drink. This is not always a choice linked to faith or culture or family expectations. Some people make the decision to be teetotal as part of a healthy lifestyle choice, some can't drink because of poor health or medication, some because they don't like the taste and some because of bad experiences with alcohol. Whatever the reason, their decision should be respected and being teetotal should always be included as an option in any social education promoting alcohol awareness.

Alcoholic beverages come in different strengths, but all contain ethanol, the correct term for pure alcohol, and tend to be divided into three general classes: beers, wines and spirits. Alcoholic drinks are made by the fermentation of fruits, grains or vegetables. Today this is usually done in sterile commercial environments, with the ideal conditions created for the alcohol to be brewed or distilled. That said, there are still plenty of people who make their own wine or beer at home, using traditional methods. There is also a rise in the number of organic suppliers who use only natural ingredients and pride themselves on being 'chemical free', meaning that they don't use toxic insecticides, herbicides, fungicides and fertilizers in the process.

Short history of alcohol

Whilst it is not known exactly when the first alcoholic drinks were made, ancient recorded history as early as the Neolithic period (10,000 BC) indicates that wine or beer has been around for tens of thousands of years. Originally likely to have been made from berries or honey, it was probably an accident when somebody discovered the altered state of being created when the fermented liquid of rotting fruit is drunk. It would seem that humans have been enjoying the taste and effects ever since.

Alcohol played an important role in early religion and worship. Today, it is still used in many religious rituals, although it is prohibited in some faiths. For example, many Christian denominations use 'sacramental' or 'communion' wine to celebrate the Eucharist and Judaism uses wine on Shabbat for Kiddush. Alternatively some faiths, including Islam, Jainism and the Seventh Day Adventist Church, restrict, discourage or forbid the consumption of alcohol for varying reasons.

Alcohol and faith is a fascinating subject, especially if you are working with a group of young people from different faiths. Consider undertaking a project to research the role of alcohol in different cultures.

Alcohol – the effects

Alcohol is a psychoactive substance that has the ability to change consciousness and alter perceptions and behaviour. In other words it is a 'mood-altering' drug that affects all parts of the body.

Although alcohol is often associated with partying and celebrations it is actually part of the group of drugs called 'depressants'. This doesn't mean that if you drink you feel depressed (although some people do) but that alcohol slows the function of the central nervous system and blocks some of the messages trying to get to the brain. This alters perceptions, emotions, movement, vision and hearing. The more you drink, the more these are affected, which is why health experts recommend safe limits.

Small amounts of alcohol can make a person feel more relaxed or less anxious. Lots of people report feeling more confident or less shy after drinking; others like the taste or the social element of pubs, etc., and for these and many more valid reasons millions of people worldwide enjoy drinking in moderation, with little or no risk to their health and wellbeing.

The more alcohol consumed the greater the changes in the brain, resulting in 'intoxication' or 'being drunk'. Once again, the effects of this stage vary between people dependent on things including their mood before drinking, their height and weight, individual tolerance to alcohol, the people they are with, the places they go and the type of alcohol consumed.

Alcohol can affect people in different ways too. Some report being more talkative, giggly and friendly, whilst others become aggressive and angry. The more consumed, the likelihood of judgement becoming impaired increases, leading to people doing things they would normally decide against or making decisions that they later regret. Physical changes can include slurred speech, difficulty in maintaining balance and lack of limb co-ordination.

Large amounts of alcohol, or 'binge drinking', defined as more than twice the recommended daily limits, especially consumed in a short space of time, can result in alcohol poisoning.[1] This includes violent vomiting and/or diarrhoea, extreme sleepiness, unconsciousness, breathing difficulties, dangerously low blood sugar, seizures, and in extreme cases death.

Drinking responsibly

Many people drink alcohol in moderation without unpleasant side-effects. The Department of Health in the UK recommends that safe drinking levels for fully grown women are 2–3 alcohol units per day and 3–4 units for men. People who drink heavily risk long-term damage to their vital organs, such as the liver, heart and brain.

The reason alcohol can cause extensive damage is because there is no cell in the body resistant to it. This means that after drinking it, alcohol can travel around the body in a way that is unstoppable. Myths such as drinking black coffee or taking a cold shower to sober up do not work – only time can allow the body to rid itself of the alcohol.

---

1 www.nhs.uk/Livewell/alcohol/Pages/Bingedrinking.aspx

When you drink alcohol it goes straight into the stomach where, without food, it is absorbed directly into the bloodstream. Food slows down the absorption of alcohol, as does fruit juice and water, which is why it is a good idea to eat before drinking anything. Vomiting, whilst unpleasant, is one of the body's defences against an alcohol overdose.

Once in the bloodstream, alcohol goes to the liver for detoxification and is finally excreted from the body. There is no way of ridding the body of alcohol once it has been drunk, despite the many myths that abound on the subject. The only thing that you can do is to wait until the liver has broken it down, at the rate of approximately one unit per hour.

There is no 'safe' level recommended for young people under the age of 18 because it is considered that their body and brain are not fully mature, and alcohol can damage both. For children and young people under 18 years of age, not drinking alcohol is the safest option.

UK and Republic of Ireland units and legal information

The legal age to buy and consume alcohol in the UK and Republic of Ireland is 18.

Alcohol is measured in units. One unit is 8g or 10ml of pure alcohol in any beverage, including wines, spirits and beers.

By law all alcoholic drinks have to state how much alcohol they contain and the number of units contained in a typical serving must be printed on bottles. This is shown in percentage of alcohol by volume, ABV. The number shows the percentage of the drink that is pure alcohol. The higher the number the more alcohol the drink contains.

Units are a way of measuring how much alcohol is consumed. As a guide:

- A small 125ml glass of wine 9% ABV = 1 unit.

- A 25ml pub measure of spirit 40% ABV = 1 unit.

- A 330ml bottle of alcopop 5% ABV = 1.7 units.

- A half-pint of ordinary strength lager/beer or cider 3.5% ABV = 1 unit.

In the Republic of Ireland, the serving size of spirits is 35.5ml or 71ml. Beer is usually served in pints or half-pints.

USA units and legal information

The legal drinking age throughout the US is 21.

Although the principles are the same as in Europe and the UK, alcohol is measured using ounces and gallons instead of metric units and alcohol by weight (ABW). The concentration of alcohol to water in beer is lower than in wine or hard liquor. However, the total amount of alcohol in a typical serving of beer (12 ounces), wine (5 ounces) and hard liquor (1.5 ounces) is the same.

In the USA heavy drinking is considered as drinking on average more than two drinks per day for men or more than one drink per day for women. Binge drinking is defined as drinking five or more drinks during a single occasion for men, or four for women.

Research suggests that excessive alcohol use is the third leading lifestyle-related cause of death for people in the US each year.[2]

Canada units and legal information

The legal drinking age in Canada is determined by each province and territory. For example, in Quebec it is 18 but in Ontario it is 19 years of age.

Canadian alcoholic beverages are measured as in the UK and most of Europe, as a percentage of alcohol by volume (ABV).

Moderate drinking for men is considered as not exceeding two units per day (27.2g/day) and not exceeding 14 units per week (190g/week). For women the daily units are the same, but it is recommended that no more than nine units should be consumed per week.

---

2   www.cdc.gov/alcohol

Australia units and legal information

The Australian government defines one unit of alcohol or a 'standard drink' as 10g (12.7ml).

The safe drinking guidelines issued to reduce the risk of harm and alcohol-related injury are the same for men and women: no more than two standard drinks on any day and no more than four standard drinks on a single occasion.

Working out the number of units

Not all drinks have the same ABV; for example, some wines are 12% and bottles of stronger lager can be 5% ABV. It also needs to be remembered that these figures are based on pub measures and not those poured at home or by young people drinking together.

To work out how many units of alcohol there are in a bottle or can of drink you need to calculate:

$$\frac{\% \text{ ABV} \times \text{the quantity in millilitres}}{1000}$$

So a 330ml bottle of lager at 5% ABV is:

$$\frac{5 \times 330}{1000} = \frac{1650}{1000} = 1.65 \text{ units}$$

TIPS FOR SAFER DRINKING

1. Before you go out, think about how you will get home. Make sure you have a plan to get home safely and inform your parents or carers what it is regardless of whether you drink alcohol or not. It is a good idea to make these decisions now before you start drinking!

2. Eat before you go out or whilst you drink to slow down the absorption of alcohol. Carbohydrates such as pasta, rice or jacket potatoes are good for this and will help stop you feeling hungry later too.

3. Decide how much you are going to drink in advance and try to stick to it. Consider going home earlier or coming out later to reduce the amount of time you will be drinking if you think this may be a problem.

4. Drink plenty of water or soft drinks to help slow down your drinking and have a glass of water before you go out so that you are not thirsty. A glass of water before you go to bed helps re-hydrate you too.

5. Know what a unit of alcohol is and how many are in your drinks. Avoid drinking from shared large bottles and mixing drinks or cocktails, as it is easy to lose track of how much you have drunk.

6. Some drinks contain more alcohol than others so consider drinking normal strength cans or bottles of drink rather than extra-strong lager or alcopops.

7. Only accept drinks from people you trust and watch to make sure you are being given what you have asked for. Don't leave drinks or bottles unattended.

8. Avoid 'binge drinking' sessions and have days in the week when you drink no alcohol at all.

9. Consider where you drink and make sure that you are not putting yourself in a risky situation where it would be difficult to get help in an emergency; for example, in a park at night.

10. Think about who you drink with and make sure that you feel safe. If you know that you will be encouraged to drink more with some friends or feel pressured into doing things you are not comfortable with, try to meet them at times you know alcohol won't be around. Alternatively make sure there are people you trust within the group and stay with them.

WARM-UPS

POUR ME A DRINK!

If you have a large group then set up two or three demonstration bottles and divide the young people into groups of four to do the exercise.

Aim

This quick activity introduces and explains the term 'unit of alcohol'.

You will need

- An empty wine bottle
- An empty vodka or gin bottle
- Clear plastic cups
- Water
- Red food colouring
- A 125ml wine glass

- A spirit measure (often freely available as the screw caps of mixer drinks)
- Flipchart and marker
- Bucket

How to do it

To prepare, fill the vodka and wine bottle with water. Add enough red food colouring to the wine bottle to make it look as though it is filled with red wine. Write up the young people's initials into a column on the flipchart paper.

Seat the young people in a circle and hand each person a clear plastic cup.

Show the young people the prepared bottles and invite them to have a drink, choosing from red wine or vodka. To avoid accidents do point out that the liquid in the bottles isn't actually alcohol. Pass the bottles around, asking each person to pour a 'standard' measure into their plastic cup.

Wait until everyone has got a 'drink' and then explain that the standard volume for one unit of alcohol for wine is 125ml and for spirits 25ml. This is usually how it is served in bars and restaurants, although some do serve glasses of wine up to 320ml and spirits in 35ml shots.

Next, taking the bucket, move around the circle inviting the young people to pour their 'drinks' into either the 125ml wine glass or the shot measure and comparing the volume of the two. Empty surplus into the bucket as you go along.

Record each person's attempt – a tick for a measure that is either just under or just over the correct amount, a double tick for anyone getting it spot on and a cross for those who do not get it right.

Once everyone's attempt has been measured review the recordings made:

1. How many people got it right?

2. How many poured more than twice the measure?

3. How did people decide how much to pour?

Now point out that although a unit of alcohol remains the same, the volume of the liquid changes due to the percentage of alcohol in the drink. Explain that the alcohol by volume (ABV) of wine, for example, can vary between 9% and 17%. This is the same for different strength lagers and ciders.

Conclude that this can contribute to making it harder to keep aware of how much alcohol you are actually consuming.

ALCOHOL BALL

If you have a large group then divide the group into two and set up two games. If the group is small then invite them all to take part.

Aim

This quick energizer demonstrates the blurred vision and poor co-ordination that can result from consuming large quantities of alcohol.

You will need

- Three tennis or juggling balls

How to do it

Invite the young people to form a seated circle and ask for a few volunteers. Ask the volunteers to come into the circle and hand them a ball, which they should start throwing to each other and catching.

Congratulate them on doing well and then throw in another ball to be passed between them and then a third. Once again remark on their hand-to-eye co-ordination skills.

Next, ask half of the volunteers to spin around ten times, pause and then spin another five times as fast as they can. Immediately the remainder of the volunteers should resume throwing the ball around the group, making sure to include the 'spinners'.

Invite the rest of the young people to observe what happens. It is likely that the 'spinners' are finding it hard to follow the ball, catch it or throw it with the same accuracy.

Call time and review the exercise, suggesting that people who drink too much alcohol have similar blurred vision and poor co-ordination.

Finish by asking:

- How could these effects impact on the life of the drinker?

- How could they impact on those around them?

CATEGORIES

This is a team game exercise to introduce the topic of alcohol.

Aim

This short game assesses young people's knowledge of alcohol.

You will need

- Piece of paper and pens for each team
- Prize (optional)

How to do it

Split the group into two teams. Explain that this is a team game and that the winning team will be the group that accumulates the most points throughout the game. Hand each group a piece of paper and a pen. Now explain that there are three rounds to the game; for each round teams should write down as many answers as they can think of.

The three rounds are:

- Names of Alcoholic Drinks
- Famous Names of Pubs in TV and Film
- Facts about Alcohol

Allow three to five minutes for each round. The team with the most qualifying answers wins.

TAKING RISKS

This session is shown as a group activity, but it is easily adapted for individual work.

Aim

This is a good way to start groups thinking about risk-taking behaviour and ways to reduce risk of harm.

You will need

- Flipchart paper
- Markers

How to do it

Ask the young people to choose a partner to work with and ask each pair to identify five risk-taking activities that are admired in our society, for example mountain climbing, skiing, sailing around the world.

When they have completed this task ask each pair to join another pair to make a four and share what they have on their lists.

Facilitate a whole-group feedback to discuss similarities and the types of activities identified. Now ask what things are done to reduce the risk of harm for people taking part in the activities down to a suitable level, for example, safety harnesses or training.

Now, ask the group to go back into their fours and consider risk-taking that may happen as a result of alcohol, for example, unprotected sex or aggressive behaviour. Ask the group to agree on five in particular and then discuss and agree things that could be done to reduce the risks.

Facilitate a group feedback session discussing the main points raised.

HOT SEAT CIRCLE

This is a good way to re-energize a group and start a session on alcohol.

Aim

This activity shares information in the group and assesses levels of knowledge.

You will need

- Nothing

How to do it

Before you start the exercise ask the young people to think of some facts with which they are familiar concerning alcohol. Explain that you are going to ask everyone in the group to share three things they know about alcohol – two will be facts and true and the third will be untrue.

Ask the young people to create a circle and ask for a volunteer to go first. They should then share their three things. The task for the rest of the group is to guess which the untruth is. The person who guesses correctly goes next.

Discuss and reinforce the truths and challenge the untruth after each round.

HANGMAN

This uses a game that most young people have played at some time. You can use it with any size group, although with large groups you are unlikely to have time for everyone to have a turn.

Aim

The idea of this version of 'hangman' is to assess the knowledge of alcohol issues in the group.

You will need

- Flipchart paper
- Markers

How to do it

Explain that you are going to play 'hangman' and that the theme for the game is alcohol. Make sure that the entire group is clear about what you are asking before you start.

Start the game off by giving an example yourself, for example, INTOXICATED or DRUNK, and put the appropriate dashes in place of letters to represent the word on a large sheet of flipchart paper.

Invite the group to take turns to call out letters, for example, 'a'. If it is in the word, write it in. If not, write the letter and draw the head of a 'stick person'. Continue making a 'stick person' with the incorrect answers, finally drawing a rectangle for a 'bed'. A guess can be made at any time, but if it is incorrect the person who guessed is 'out' and cannot make any further attempts for that turn.

The person who solves the puzzle correctly goes next and sets their own task for the group to solve.

ALCOHOL WORDSEARCH

This is another warm-up that uses a format that most young people know so it requires little explanation.

Aim

To open up discussions around alcohol and encourage young people to work together.

You will need

- Copies of the wordsearch enlarged to A3 size
- Coloured felt pens
- Prize (optional)

How to do it

Divide the young people into groups of three and hand each group an A3 copy of the wordsearch and a coloured felt pen.

Explain that the task is to complete the wordsearch as quickly as possible. First group finished wins!

Review the activity making sure that the young people are clear about the meaning of the terms used and explaining if they aren't.

Alcohol wordsearch

U	N	I	T	C	V	E	E	G	N	I	B	E	E
I	Q	E	A	X	T	E	D	I	C	I	L	J	R
A	N	T	I	S	O	C	I	A	L	M	O	S	S
O	P	G	L	A	G	E	R	N	P	N	O	C	T
E	S	S	I	D	E	R	K	N	U	R	D	I	D
I	V	B	V	M	M	H	J	K	H	W	S	D	E
G	S	D	E	P	R	E	S	S	A	N	T	E	T
H	X	S	R	S	P	I	S	T	N	B	R	R	A
T	N	I	P	D	S	C	F	B	G	F	E	I	C
E	E	R	T	A	L	C	O	P	O	P	A	U	I
E	A	B	O	O	Z	E	Z	E	V	D	M	R	X
N	I	Y	L	J	P	W	U	C	E	C	C	T	O
R	K	H	D	E	T	N	E	M	R	E	F	O	T
O	T	R	R	K	F	S	P	I	R	I	T	O	N
L	A	N	D	L	O	R	D	S	I	Z	M	L	I

Search to find the following alcohol-related words:

Unit	Eighteen
Booze	Lager
Binge	Fermented
Depressant	Pint
Hangover	Spirit
Alcopop	Liver
Intoxicated	Cider
Drunk	Bloodstream
Antisocial	Landlord

COPYRIGHT © VANESSA ROGERS 2012

DID YOU KNOW?

This quiz is shown as a group activity, but is easily adapted for one-to-one work.

Aim

This activity encourages young people to share the information they have about a range of alcohol-related issues. It is also an assessment tool for facilitators to understand the level of knowledge in the group.

You will need

- Large sheets of paper
- Markers
- Prize (optional)

How to do it

Divide the young people into teams and explain that this exercise is a quiz, requiring 'yes' or 'no' answers. Although they will get a point for each correct answer, they will get additional points for every correct fact that they can add to support it. The team with the most points wins!

Slowly ask the questions allowing time for team discussion. At the end, facilitate a round robin where each team offers the answer to one question. After this the other teams can chip in with further facts and information.

Mark the team scores up as you go along. When the last question has been covered add up the scores and lead a round of applause for the team which has the most points.

DID YOU KNOW? QUESTIONS

1. Does a shot of whisky have about the same amount of alcohol in it as a regular half-pint of beer?

   Yes, they both contain approximately one unit of alcohol, even though the volume of liquid is different.

2. Do some cans of strong lager contain more alcohol than three single shots of vodka?

   Yes, premium high strength lagers and ciders can have up to 3.5 units in a single can. This means that if two people drink three rounds together, one drinking cans of strong cider and the other standard 25ml shots of vodka, the

person drinking the cider will have consumed 10.5 units of alcohol, whilst the person drinking vodka will have had 3 units.

3. Can giving up drinking alcohol or cutting back quickly make you feel unwell?
    Yes, heavy drinkers who have drunk regularly over a long period may feel bad and experience serious physical withdrawal symptoms if they suddenly quit. These can include:

    - feeling jumpy and nervous
    - having sleep problems
    - having body tremors (the 'shakes')
    - seizures
    - hallucinations.

    It is important to get professional advice and support if someone is serious about tackling alcohol-related problems.

4. Do some people get more drunk than others on the same amount of alcohol?
    Yes, because of lots of factors including weight, height, ethnicity and even gender. As a general rule, if a woman and a man of the same weight drink the same amount of alcohol under the exact same circumstances, the woman will on average have a much higher BAC (Blood Alcohol Content) than the man.

This is because women have much less of an enzyme called alcohol dehydrogenase in their stomachs than men do. There is also evidence to suggest that alcohol tolerance changes at different points in a woman's menstrual cycle, making her more vulnerable to the effects in the days leading up to her period.

5. If a woman is drinking alcohol whilst breastfeeding will her baby consume alcohol too?

   Yes, alcohol can be passed to her baby through the milk. This may affect the baby's feeding, its sleep and how it develops. If the mother does drink, even in moderation, she should feed the baby or pump breast milk beforehand.

6. Is it dangerous to mix alcohol with other drugs?

   Yes, it can be dangerous and even fatal to mix drugs, including prescription or over-the-counter remedies. If you mix some over-the-counter drugs, such as flu remedies, with alcohol your body may react violently. Some combinations of prescribed drugs and alcohol can make you vomit, have cramps or even have breathing difficulties. The thing to remember is that alcohol and other drugs just do not mix.

   Where illegal drugs are concerned the dangers increase, because you don't know the exact ingredients of the dosage. As well as any chemical reactions that occur when two substances are mixed, drinking and smoking cannabis or popping club drugs can increase the likelihood of getting into dangerous situations and can lead to decisions that may be regretted later.

7. Name at least six physical effects on the body of long-term drinking.
    These could include:

    - **high blood pressure**
    - **strokes**
    - **brain damage**
    - **nerve damage**
    - **reduced interest in sex**
    - **low sex hormone levels**
    - **liver disease**
    - **alcohol dependence**
    - **complication in pregnancy**
    - **damage to unborn foetus**
    - **diseases of the stomach and digestive system**
    - **ulcers.**

NAME THE COUNTRY

This activity can be developed into looking at the global alcohol industry.

Aim

This quick quiz introduces the notion that alcohol is a worldwide industry and looks at the drinks associated with different countries.

You will need

- Paper
- Pens

How to do it

Decide if you are going to facilitate this as a team or individual quiz and set up accordingly with paper and pens.

Suggest that some drinks are associated with different countries in the world, either because it is where it originates from or because it is where the most famous brands are still brewed or fermented.

Explain that you are going to read out a list of names of alcoholic drinks, not brands, and the task is to write down the country that they think is most associated with each. You can add your own suggestions that use brand names; for example, a well-known stout brewed in Ireland, or local popular drinks.

Once you have gone through the list go back and give the answers, asking the young people to add up their scores as they go along. The team or person with the most correct answers wins!

Reflect on the answers:

- Were there any surprises?

- What might be the reasons that different drinks were originally made in different countries?

Discuss ecological things that might impact on the drinks made. For example, tequila is a spirit made from the blue agave plant, which is found primarily in the area surrounding the city of Tequila in Mexico. It does not grow naturally in Kent in England, but hops do, which are used in ale brewing.

Conclude that humans have for tens of thousands of years fermented and brewed alcohol, originally using the plants, fruits and vegetables that they found growing locally. Regional specialities were developed and some places are still heavily associated with the alcohol that they produce, for example, the Champagne region in France.

Over time people travelled more and brought back plants, developed irrigation systems and discovered ways to greenhouse fruits that would otherwise die in less temperate climates. This meant that they could experiment with their own versions of regional drinks and now alcohol is fermented and produced commercially almost worldwide. So, although gin is traditionally associated with Holland, Britain is currently one of the world's largest producers of it.

DRINKS AND ASSOCIATED COUNTRIES

Ouzo	Greece
Bourbon	USA
Lager	Germany
Vodka	Russia

Tequila	Mexico
Wine	France
Brandy	Spain
Sake	Japan
Gin	Holland
Sherry	Spain
Whisky	Scotland
Brown ale	England
Alcopop	Australia

ACTIVITIES

EXPLORING POSITIVE AND NEGATIVE PEER PRESSURE

Aim

This discussion-based activity enables young people to explore the positive and negative power of collective and peer pressure.

You will need

- Flipchart paper
- Markers

How to do it

Invite the young people to reflect on all of the groups to which they belong. This should include friendship groups and families as well as organized groups such as sports clubs or uniformed groups such as the Scouts or Guides. Discuss the positive feelings and benefits they get from membership. This could include love, security, shared interests, fun and a sense of 'belonging'.

Now move on to ask:

- Do you behave the same way in a group as you do on your own?
- Do you behave differently with different groups?

Discuss the differences in behaviour, for example, between being at a party with friends and at a family celebration with grandparents. Conclude that most people are multi-faceted and show different sides of themselves in different circumstances. Explain that psychologists' research suggests people are heavily influenced by the people they spend time with and what they see others doing.

Discuss, in pairs, a time when:

- you were encouraged by others to succeed in something you found challenging
- you felt pressured by others into doing something you believe to be wrong.

Encourage the young people to explore the reasons behind their actions and what informed their final decisions, including what they hoped to gain or feared to lose by their choices.

Invite feedback and record ideas under the headings 'GAIN' and 'LOSE'. So, for example, a gain might be achievement, satisfaction, peer acceptance or status, but by following the crowd you may lose respect, get into trouble, feel guilty or lose the opportunity to act on your values.

Explain that the factors that persuade someone to do, or not do, something can be referred to as the risk and protective factors that contribute to 'peer pressure'. Whilst belonging to a group can create powerful feelings of safety, protection and value, peer pressure can sway people to engage in less positive behaviour as well and even get swept along into actions they later regret. This includes decisions about alcohol; for example, what to drink, when to drink and how much.

Conclude that whilst it can be hard to go against the crowd it is important to maintain personal values and remain an individual within a group. Peer pressure, whilst powerful, should not be used as an excuse for making negative choices as everyone has personal responsibility for their decisions and actions, as well as responsibilities to the groups of which they are a part.

HAVE A DRINK!

Aim

This activity considers peer pressure and some of the arguments used to encourage people to drink alcohol to help develop assertiveness skills.

You will need

- A copy of the 'Have a Drink!' cards

How to do it

Ask the young people to form two circles, one inside the other, checking that each person has someone standing opposite them.

Hand each member of the inside circle a 'Have a Drink!' card, asking them not to show anyone else what is on it.

When you say 'Go!' they should begin a conversation with the person standing opposite them, beginning with 'Have a drink...' followed by the argument on their card. They then have two minutes to put as much pressure as possible on their partner to persuade them to have an alcoholic drink. The person being pressured should do their best to resist and offer counter-arguments to support their standpoint.

After two minutes, call time and ask each person in the outer circle to take a step to their left. They now have a new partner who will offer another reason to have a drink. Once again, they have two minutes to put pressure on to drink.

Repeat the exercise until the young people have gone full circle and returned to their original partner.

Ask the two circles of young people to form two groups and ask each to discuss:

1. How did it feel to put pressure on someone to drink or be pressured into drinking alcohol?

2. Which arguments were the most compelling?

3. In real life, what other arguments might be used to encourage someone to drink?

Bring the two groups back together and share views, especially focusing on how easy or difficult it was to resist this kind of peer pressure and the factors that made them decide to accept or not accept the invitation to 'Have a drink'.

Discuss real-life arguments that may have been used to encourage drinking and consider the most effective strategies for assertively making personal choices.

Conclude that for most cultures adults drinking alcohol responsibly, particularly in social settings, is an acceptable thing to do. This makes many of the arguments to drink all the more compelling, unlike other drugs and controlled substances, which have legal consequences, and where social acceptance is generally much lower. However, the choice of whether or not to drink alcohol, at any age, should be a personal one so it is important to develop the skills to be assertive in situations where peer pressure may make it difficult to make healthy choices.

'Have a Drink!' cards

…it's good for your heart, that's a medical fact	…it will give you extra confidence
…everyone else will have been drinking so we need to catch up	…you've had a stressful day and it'll help you relax
…otherwise you won't enjoy the party	…vodka is low in calories so you won't put on weight

COPYRIGHT © VANESSA ROGERS 2012

…don't be boring!	…it's antisocial not to
…what do you mean, 'you don't drink'?	…you know you want to!
…go on, everybody else is drinking	…it's vodka, so you can't smell it
…no one is going to find out	…one drink won't hurt you

COPYRIGHT © VANESSA ROGERS 2012

INFLUENCING

This is a small-group activity that will need clear boundaries to ensure individuals feel safe to participate.

Aim

To practise influencing and negotiating skills and open up discussions around peer pressure.

You will need

- Copies of the 'Influencing' cards

How to do it

Divide the group into threes and explain that two of them will take turns to be the 'influencer', whilst the third is an observer.

Hand each 'influencer' a card. The influencers should try to influence the other person, using the subject on the card as the goal, into doing what they ask. The person being 'influenced' should try to resist all persuasion. The observer should make a note of how many times the influencer made a statement (gave information), how many times they asked a question (sought information) and how many times they offered a reason to do as they suggested (peer pressure).

After five minutes stop and ask the participants to listen to observer feedback.

Swap cards and roles until everyone has had the opportunity to experience influencing, observing and being pressured.

Facilitate a whole-group discussion that looks at the different styles people adopted to persuade each other and how easy or difficult it was to resist this. Note down key factors that persuaded young people to go along with whatever was suggested, and those that helped them maintain their position and not be persuaded.

'Influencing' cards

Encourage your friend to attempt to buy alcohol, even though they are under-age	Encourage your friend to accept a lift home, even though the driver has been drinking
Encourage your friend to steal alcohol from home to take to a party	Encourage your friend to use fake ID to get into a club
Encourage your friend to have an alcoholic drink at a family wedding	Encourage your friend to have alcohol at a party whilst their parents are away

COPYRIGHT © VANESSA ROGERS 2012

Encourage your friend to text their ex after drinking	Encourage your friend to stay out drinking later than their curfew
Encourage your friend to support you in an argument when you have both been drinking	Encourage your friend to take a short cut home at night after drinking

COPYRIGHT © VANESSA ROGERS 2012

MORE LIKELY, LESS LIKELY

To adapt this for less physically able young people use red and green cards to show choices and facilitate the activity seated.

Aim

This is a 'feet first' activity that explores the situations in which young people are more or less likely to drink alcohol, and the reasons why.

You will need

- Flipchart
- Marker

How to do it

Start the activity by suggesting that lots of things impact on people's decision to drink, or not to drink, alcohol.

These include:

- what their friends do
- what their family does
- faith and culture
- media influences
- the cost of alcohol
- where they are.

Explain that this session is going to look at how where you are, sometimes referred to as the 'setting', can impact on your decisions about alcohol.

Read out the following list of places and occasions where an opportunity to drink alcohol is available. After each the young people should move either to the left-hand side of the room, indicating that they think they would be 'More Likely' to drink, or the right-hand side, meaning they are 'Less Likely' to drink.

After each round ask the young people to explain their decisions and on the flipchart paper record the contributing factors under the headings 'More Likely' and 'Less Likely'. So, for example, a young person may say they are more likely to drink alcohol at a family party because they feel safe, it is free and other members of their family have offered it to them. Equally another young person may say they are less likely to drink at a family wedding because of their family culture, because their parents would disapprove or because they don't feel comfortable.

Finally, bring the young people back together and review the points you have noted throughout the activity. Invite suggestions and discuss other factors that make alcohol consumption more or less likely.

Conclude that how you feel about the 'settings' where alcohol is offered, as well as the people who are with you, has a huge impact on the decisions you make.

MORE OR LESS LIKELY?

1. At a family party
2. In the park with friends
3. At home with parents
4. At a house party
5. On a school trip
6. On a youth club weekend away
7. On a camping trip with friends
8. At a family BBQ
9. With a meal at home
10. On a night out with friends
11. At school or college
12. In a friend's bedroom

WHY DRINK?

This session works equally well as a group or individual activity.

Aim

This is a sorting activity to explore the reasons why people choose to drink alcohol.

You will need

- Enough sets of the 'Why Drink?' cards for the young people to work in small groups

How to do it

Pose the question, 'Why do people drink alcohol?'

Divide the young people into groups of four and hand each a set of the 'Why Drink?' cards. Explain that these are a selection of common reasons that people give for choosing to drink. Stress that the list is not exhaustive and that there will be time later to share any other ideas they may have.

The task is to read and discuss the cards and then rank them from the reason that they think is most popular, through to the reason that they think is the least popular. These should then be placed to make a diamond shape, with the top reason at one end, and the least at the other.

When every group has finished, invite them to share and compare their findings.

Encourage debate about the different reasons given and invite any additional reasons that the young people have heard given for a decision to drink alcohol.

'Why Drink?' cards

TO GET DRUNK	TO FEEL GOOD	TO REDUCE STRESS
TO RELAX	TO FEEL MORE CONFIDENT	TO GET IN THE MOOD
TO CELEBRATE	CURIOSITY	TO FORGET PROBLEMS

COPYRIGHT © VANESSA ROGERS 2012

TO FEEL MORE ATTRACTIVE	BECAUSE IT TASTES GOOD	TO ESCAPE REAL LIFE
TO OVERCOME SHYNESS	TO FEEL ROMANTIC	TO FEEL COMFORTABLE IN SOCIAL SETTINGS
TO FIT IN	TO BE SOCIABLE	TO HAVE FUN

COPYRIGHT © VANESSA ROGERS 2012

ALCOHOL VALUES MAPS

You can do this as an individual piece of work or as a group task. Find out in advance if there are any specific issues within the group so that you can decide if it is appropriate.

Aim

To encourage young people to consider the impact cultural and family values have on personal attitudes to alcohol.

You will need

- A4 sheets of paper
- Pens

How to do it

Hand a sheet of paper and a pen to each young person. Explain that for the moment you would like them to work alone, although you will be inviting them to talk later. This gives them the opportunity to decide how much they want to share.

Explain that the task is to draw a family tree that shows two generations. You could draw a simple family tree on flipchart paper so that they can see what you mean.

Against the name of each family member they should indicate if this person drinks, or has ever drunk, alcohol and then write any messages given by them about alcohol. This can include any unspoken family or cultural values or factual information given, as well as messages received by observing behaviour and attitudes to drinking; for example, being told that red wine is good for you but witnessing adult hangovers!

Now ask the young people to add friends or other members of their community to the values map with the messages about alcohol they picked up from them. Are they different?

Once they have completed this, invite the young people to discuss their findings with the person sitting next to them. Encourage them to reflect on how the messages they received impact on how they view alcohol consumption now.

Feed back the main points from the different discussions into the main group, pulling out any issues for further work.

ALCOHOL DRAMA

This exercise works best with a small group of young people who know each other well enough to be relaxed and participate fully.

Aim

This activity looks at the positives and negatives of drinking alcohol.

You will need

- Small plastic cups
- Soft drink
- Two flipchart sheets
- Markers

Set up a 'bar' area. This is now the stage. Ask for a young person to volunteer as the bar tender. They should give each young person a drink as they come to the bar and the young people then 'act' the effects of the alcohol. Start them in pairs if you think they will be nervous.

As each effect is acted out, ask two note-writers to write up the effects. Usually there are more negatives than positives. Once they have finished, turn around the flipcharts and draw a smiley face next to positives and a sad face next to the negatives. Positives could include relaxation, feeling more confident or to celebrate. Negatives could include being sick, weight gain or liver damage.

Look at the flipcharts and add additional points if needed. If the negatives outweigh the positives ask the young people why people drink alcohol and facilitate a discussion. Ask them how they could achieve the positives without alcohol and record for future use.

MIXED MESSAGES

This activity explores the messages that young people receive about alcohol that contribute to developing their own set of values and attitudes.

Aim

For young people to consider the range and quality of information they receive about alcohol.

You will need

- Three large flipchart sheets headed 'FAMILY', 'FRIENDS' and 'MEDIA'
- Markers

How to do it

Divide the main group into three smaller groups. Start off by asking the young people to say where they first heard about alcohol from. Acknowledge that there are many different messages about alcohol from friends, parents, TV, films and advertising and that these are not always the same.

Hand each small group a headed flipchart sheet and some markers, explaining that they each have a different heading to look at. Then ask them to discuss and record all the things that they have heard or the messages they have received about alcohol from the group on their sheet. Allow 10 to 15 minutes for the task and then invite each group to feed back.

Facilitate a discussion that looks at the findings and challenges any myths, stereotypes or incorrect information. Which source has the biggest influence on decisions they make about alcohol?

WHAT'S IN A DRINK?

This is shown as a group activity but adapts well for one-to-one work. It can be adapted to include drinks that are familiar to the young people with whom you are working.

Aim

This activity encourages young people to start thinking about what ingredients are used in an alcoholic drink.

You will need

- Photocopied sets of the drinks cards
- Envelopes
- Internet access
- Paper
- Pens

How to do it

Divide the large group into small groups of three or four. Hand each group an envelope containing a copy of the cards cut up and shuffled.

Explain that the task is to match the ingredient with the correct alcoholic drink. Stress that it doesn't matter if people aren't sure – there is no expectation that everyone will get all the answers right.

Allow five to ten minutes for discussion and completion and then go through the answers. Encourage the young people to question, challenge or add information as you go along.

Talk through the cards one more time to reinforce learning and then set the young people, in pairs, the task of choosing an alcoholic beverage and then researching online the ingredients. At this stage each pair should keep their choice secret.

Once everyone has finished their research they should join together to form a seated circle. Each pair should now introduce the ingredient they have been researching and allow the rest of the group to guess which alcoholic drink it is found in.

Drinks cards

GIN	**JUNIPER BERRIES**
VODKA	**POTATOES**
WHISKY	**RYE**
CIDER	**APPLES**

COPYRIGHT © VANESSA ROGERS 2012

SAKE	RICE
WINE	GRAPES
RUM	SUGAR CANE
TEQUILA	BLUE AGAVE PLANT

COPYRIGHT © VANESSA ROGERS 2012

IF I MADE THE LAW

This is shown as a group activity but adapts well for one-to-one work. Check the laws for your country or state online to discuss later.

Aim

This activity checks out young people's values and attitudes to the laws that control the sale of alcohol.

You will need

- Large sheets of paper
- Coloured markers

How to do it

Divide the large group into small groups of three or four and give each group paper and pens.

Start by asking the young people to call out any laws or legal restrictions of which they are aware regarding the control of selling alcohol; for example, the legal age for purchasing it. Note these down where the young people can see them to refer to later.

Do a quick poll by asking for a show of hands to see who supports the current legal age to buy and consume alcohol on licensed premises.

Now ask the young people to discuss in their small groups any laws that they would bring in, change or amend if they were in a position to do so. Suggest that whilst making their decisions they consider the impact alcohol has on:

- individuals
- families
- communities
- government (e.g. tax revenue).

Ask that they make notes to help them present their ideas later.

Allow 20 minutes for discussion and completion and then invite each group to present their 'laws' that they would make to control the sale of alcohol. Encourage the young people to question, challenge or add information as you go along.

Finally facilitate a short discussion that reflects the young people's views on the laws that currently govern where they live. Do they agree with them? If not, encourage them to research online the process for making and changing laws and consider developing this into a larger project that can look at the health, financial and social implications of any proposed changes.

SOCIETY – WHO DOES ALCOHOL HARM MOST?

This is a small-group exercise that can be adapted for individual work.

Aim

This sorting activity opens up discussions around the wider harm that alcohol can cause in communities.

You will need

- Paper and a red, green and orange marker for each group of four
- Flipchart paper and a marker

How to do it

Divide the young people into groups of four and hand each group paper and a red, green and orange marker pen.

Demonstrate drawing a traffic light on flipchart paper and ask each group to draw their own on the paper.

Explain that you are going to read out some scenarios of things that a young person might do or cause to happen whilst drunk. They should decide whether they think it is red – extremely harmful, amber – harmful, green – not harmful and then write the scenario number in the appropriate traffic light.

Once all of the scenarios have been read and placed, go through them together stopping to discuss different choices and the reasons behind the choices made.

Discuss:

- What harm might these actions cause?

- Who to?

- What long-term consequences might there be?

Conclude that heavy drinking can cause harm to more than just the health of the person who has made the decision to become intoxicated. It can have a knock-on effect too; for example, a pensioner out walking his dog is frightened by encountering a drunken teenager, he tells his friends what has happened and they too become worried about leaving their homes after dark. This leads to a loss of independence, which means that their family has to offer more support and lifts to places they would once have walked to. This makes family members resentful of the drunken young person and wary of other young people. One of the family members is a councillor and due to this experience he becomes prejudiced towards young people so that when the local youth club runs short of funds, he votes to shut it.

SCENARIOS

1. Their unborn child
2. Their boss when they call in sick due to a hangover
3. The drinker
4. The pensioner they scare
5. The friend they embarrass
6. The toilet cleaner who has to clean up their vomit
7. The person they knock down whilst driving
8. The police who are called
9. The bar owner whose glass they break
10. The people who live near pubs/clubs
11. The taxi driver they abuse
12. Their victim of aggressive behaviour
13. The neighbour whose garden they urinate in
14. The supermarket whose trolley they steal

15. The person they sing at in the street
16. The person they assault
17. The person in the takeaway restaurant they racially abuse
18. The bar person they make obscene suggestions to
19. The nurse in A&E they shout at
20. The partner they cheat on

BOTTLES

This activity opens up discussion around units of alcohol and assesses young people's knowledge.

Aim

To correctly guess the number of alcoholic units in well-known drinks.

You will need

- A good selection of empty cans and bottles of alcoholic drinks
- Sticky labels
- Markers
- A table to use as a 'bar'

How to do it

In advance collect the empty bottles and cans and place labels under each to show how many units of alcohol they contain. These will have their unit content displayed somewhere, so block this out with a permanent black marker. Now set up your 'bar' area with the bottles and cans arranged on it.

Invite young people to go to the bar, choose a drink and guess how many units they think it contains. Ask the rest of the group to indicate if they think the answer is higher or lower than the guess – be as theatrical as you like for this!

Turn the can or bottle over to reveal the answer.

Keep going until all the examples have been guessed and then facilitate a discussion over the findings. Did the young people realize the alcoholic contents of the drinks? Reinforce safe drinking levels.

ALCOHOL BODY MAP

This activity works with groups of up to six young people. You do need to be sensitive to gender and personal space boundaries when facilitating whose outline is being drawn and by whom.

Aim

To produce a map that shows the long-term and short-term effects of alcohol on the body.

You will need

- A very large sheet of paper
- Assortment of marker pens
- Blu-Tack
- Photocopy of Alcohol Body Map sheet
- Scissors

How to do it

Before the group arrives, photocopy the Alcohol Body Map sheet and cut into rectangles.

Lay the large sheet out on the floor in the middle of the group. Ask one of the young people to volunteer to lie flat on the paper and be drawn around by another member of the group. This part will need to be facilitated carefully.

Once they have finished ask the 'template' to stand up. You should now have a life-size human silhouette to work with!

Now, with the template still in the middle, place the slips with the potential results of alcohol use face down onto the 'body'. Before you ask the group to do anything else, make sure that you explain that this is not what will happen to every person who ever drinks any alcohol, but that these are potential effects of alcohol use/misuse. This may be a good time to reinforce safe drinking levels.

After you have explained this, invite the group to take it in turns to take a piece of Blu-Tack and stick each label in the correct place on the body.

When all the labels are on the body, facilitate a group discussion around the process. Are all the labels in the right place? If not, ask if anyone else has an idea where they should be and encourage the group to work together to agree a final 'body map'.

Finally ask the young people to use two different coloured pens to indicate which of the effects are long-term and which are short-term.

Once all the labels are in the right place you can use the body map as a discussion point to look at some of the effects shown on the labels. Revisit any ground rules you have around confidentiality so that the group can share thoughts and knowledge, but be aware of any potential child protection issues.

Encourage the young people to consider some of the potential consequences of drinking too much alcohol, reflecting on their own experiences; for example, aggressive behaviour or getting into trouble with parents for coming home drunk. Discuss the increased risks of people having unprotected sex whilst drunk and agree some strategies to reduce risks if you are planning to drink alcohol.

Alcohol Body Map sheet

CIRRHOSIS OF THE LIVER	CANCER OF THE OESOPHAGUS
HEART DISEASE	OBESITY
HEPATITIS	DAMAGED MENTAL CAPACITY
GASTRIC ULCERS	MALNOURISHMENT
SHRINKAGE OF THE OVARIES	CANCER OF THE MOUTH
SHRINKAGE OF THE PENIS AND TESTICLES	A BAD HEADACHE
REDUCED DRIVING ABILITY	SLURRED SPEECH
BEING SICK	LESSENING OF INHIBITIONS
LOSS OF CO-ORDINATION	CRYING

COPYRIGHT © VANESSA ROGERS 2012

CONTROL MEASURES DISCUSSION

This can be used as a discussion topic for small or large groups.

Aim

To discuss existing control measures in place to prevent drivers drinking alcohol over the legal limit, and suggest new ideas.

You will need

- Paper
- Pens

How to do it

Open the session by asking young people what they think stops drivers using their cars if they have drunk more alcohol than the legal limit for driving. This could include things such as fear of hurting someone, fear of getting caught by the police or personal beliefs around alcohol.

Move the conversation on to control measures already put in place; for example, the drink–drive limit and breathalysers.

Now suggest a new form of control and tell the group about the Alcolock. Make sure you remain neutral in your presentation.

Divide the young people into two groups and hand out paper to make notes on. Group one should discuss and formulate arguments that suggest this control measure is a good idea and should become standard for all cars. Group two should discuss and formulate arguments that state that it is not a good idea and should be scrapped. Allow 20 minutes to half an hour for this and then invite the two groups back, seated opposite each other.

Facilitate a discussion that looks at both points of view and draw out final conclusions.

- Does this gadget take away personal responsibility for not drinking when driving?

- If the machine stopped working, would that be a valid excuse if a person was caught driving over the limit?

BACKGROUND INFORMATION
The Alcolock is an electronic breathalyser/immobilizer designed to stop a driver from starting the car if they have drunk more than the legal limit of alcohol. It fits on the steering

wheel and is connected to the ignition, and incorporates voice recognition technology (the driver has to hum) to prevent someone else providing a breath sample. If the test shows that the driver has more than the legal limit of 35 micrograms of alcohol per 100 millilitres of breath, the car will not start. Once the car is in motion, an electronic voice tells the driver to pull over and be re-tested at regular intervals.

UNDERSTANDING UNITS

If you have a large group consider collecting enough equipment to do more than one experiment to demonstrate with.

Aim

This is an exercise that enables young people to visualize 'units' of alcohol and understand that various alcoholic drinks can contain the same amount of alcohol, even though the serving size may be different.

You will need

- Three clear, clean empty plastic two-litre soda bottles (with lids)
- One clear, clean empty half-pint beer glass
- One clear, clean empty small wine glass (125ml)
- One clear, clean empty shot glass
- Cold water

- A teaspoon
- Red food colouring
- A tray

How to do it

To prepare for the session fill the two-litre bottles approximately three-quarters full with cold water. Make sure that the amount of liquid in the bottles is equal. You need to leave enough room for an extra half-pint of liquid to be poured in later.

Take the three empty glasses and put a measure of two teaspoons of food colouring into each glass. Fill the remainder of the glass to the serving measure marked on the side with cold water and put on the tray. You should see a clear difference in colour between the three 'drinks'.

When the young people arrive, bring out the tray and show them the three drinks on it. Explain that the liquid used for demonstrating is only water and food colouring. Introduce the half-pint glass as 'lager', the wine glass as 'red wine' and the shot glass as 'spirits' or 'hard liquor'.

Invite comments on how different the liquid in each glass looks and then ask the young people which 'drink' they think contains the most alcohol. At this stage note differences of opinions, but do not give the right answers. Conclude that the drinks have different volumes of liquid, and that the red colour varies in shade among the different drinks.

Now, bring out the three soda bottles. Invite the young people to guess what they think will happen when you add one of the 'drinks' to each of the bottles.

Ask for three volunteers. The first should pour the 'hard liquor' into the first bottle, screw on the lid and shake hard to mix. The second should take the glass of 'wine' and again pour it into a bottle, screw the lid on and shake. The final volunteer should take the half-pint glass of 'lager' and pour into the remaining bottle and repeat. Top up any remaining space in the soda bottles with water. Tell them that this experiment simulates what happens to alcohol when it mixes with water in the body.

Because each glass contains the same two teaspoons of diluted red food colouring, the shade of red in each should now be about the same.

Point out that all of the drinks contain one unit of alcohol. The bottles demonstrate the difference in the concentration of alcohol in each of the drinks. Point out that beer has the lowest concentration of alcohol, wine an intermediate concentration, and hard liquor/spirits the highest. So by drinking half a pint of normal strength beer or cider you are consuming the same amount of alcohol as a small glass of wine or a shot of spirits.

ALCOHOL AND GENDER

This activity works well with either a mixed or single gender group.

Aim

The aim of the session is to look at messages in advertisements for alcohol about gender and relationships.

You will need

- A good selection of women's and men's magazines (including those aimed at gay and lesbian people)

How to do it

Start with a short discussion about what 'stereotypes' are to make sure there is a common understanding in the group.

Suggest that advertising can reinforce these stereotypes. Ask young people for advertisements they have seen that show males or females in a stereotypical way. Encourage them to think not just of adverts on television but also in other places they have seen alcohol promoted; for example, at the cinema or in shops.

What do the adverts show? For example, are men shown to be more attractive to women, do the women wear beautiful designer clothes? Are people shown to be sexy and having fun if they drink this product? Are they shown as rich and successful? Are the messages different for men and women? Who do you think are the advertisers' intended group(s)?

Now look at the relationships shown between men and women in the adverts – are they happy? What are the couples doing? Celebrating? Being romantic? Are they sexually attracted to each other? How true are the myths that the adverts show?

Divide the group into smaller groups of three or four and ask them to design a short TV 'advert' aimed at either men or women to show 'real-life' situations that show the negative side of alcohol. For example:

- being on a date, drinking too much and being sick in front of them

- having unprotected sex

- drinking too much and getting into a fight.

Invite each group to perform their advert, encouraging applause and comments after each one.

ALCOHOL AND THE MEDIA

Aim

This activity encourages young people to consider the impact advertising has on their choices around alcohol.

You will need

- A set of advertising cards
- Flipchart paper
- Markers

How to do it

As a whole group invite the young people to call out all the brand names of alcoholic drinks that they can think of and record them on the flipchart. Reinforce that you are not asking which, if any, of these they have drunk. Then ask the young people, 'What image do these drinks have?'

Point out that under the advertising code of practice alcoholic drinks must not be packaged to appeal to under-18s (in the UK). What do the young people think about this?

Move on to suggest that alcohol companies spend vast sums of money each year to advertise and promote their products. Ask the young people if they think that images associated with brands influence them in any way. Hand out the cards and flipchart paper with markers and divide the young people into threes. Ask them to discuss each of the cards and to record how, if at all, the messages they receive have influenced their decisions to drink or not.

As a whole group facilitate a discussion that picks out points from each group. Encourage constructive challenging and questions. Pull together conclusions.

Advertising cards

TV ADVERTS	**POSTERS**
PROMOTIONAL STANDS AT FESTIVALS	**PACKAGING AND LOGOS**
PROMOTIONAL GOODS	**BILLBOARDS**
MEDIA/SPORTS/ROCK STAR ENDORSEMENT	**ONLINE ADVERTISING**

COPYRIGHT © VANESSA ROGERS 2012

HELPING HAND

To adapt this activity for mixed-ability groups use thumbs up and down signals rather than moving around the room.

Aim

This activity looks at the moral dilemmas of supporting a friend who has had too much to drink.

You will need

- Flipchart paper
- Markers

How to do it

Create an imaginary line on the floor. Label one end of the line 'HELPFUL'; the other end 'UNHELPFUL'; and 'DEPENDS' in the middle.

Explain that you want the young people to imagine that they are at a party with a good friend. Everyone has had a good time but your friend has had too much to drink and is behaving in an out-of-character way, becoming in turn aggressive and tearful. You want to help, but you are not sure what to do and you are frightened that things are going to go horribly wrong.

Now read out the suggestions of help below. Tell the young people that after each one you want them to go and stand along the imaginary line in the place that corresponds best with their opinion.

1. Call your friend's parents.

2. Take your friend outside to get some air.

3. Make your friend drink black coffee to sober up.

4. Tell your friend to make themself vomit to get rid of the alcohol.

5. Give them a glass of water to sip.

6. Call an ambulance.

7. Tell them to lie down and go to sleep.

8. Insist they leave the party and go home.

9. Do nothing – it's their problem.

10. Encourage them to sit quietly and talk to you.

11. Laugh and encourage them to do outrageous things.

12. Get angry – they have ruined the party for you.

WOULD HAVE/SHOULD HAVE

This is a small-group activity that can easily be adapted for individual work. It looks at attitudes and values and as such any group rules or contract should be referred to before you start.

Aim

To consider the differences between what people do and what they think they should do in a range of alcohol-related circumstances.

You will need

- A copy of the 'Would have/Should have' scenarios sheet for each pair
- Pens

How to do it

Ask the young people if they can think of a time when they were in a difficult situation and made a decision and acted against their principles; for example, witnessing but not challenging a bully. Conclude that sometimes we know what we should do but we do something different.

Divide the main group into smaller groups of twos or threes. Hand each group a copy of the scenarios sheet for them to discuss and make notes on. Make the point that for some scenarios what you should and would do may be the same thing. Allow 15 minutes and then bring the whole group together again.

Invite each small group to share one scenario and their agreements on what they would and should do in the circumstances. Encourage comment and invite the rest of the young people to voice their opinions.

Facilitate a discussion that considers:

1.   Why are some of the scenarios easier to deal with than others?

2.   What are the possible consequences for making the 'wrong' or the 'right' decision?

3.   What helps in the decision-making process?

'Would have/Should have' scenarios

SCENARIO 1

Your best friend Jamie has been selling cheap beer at school that he steals from his parents' pub. Today he sells two cans of strong lager to one of the younger girls and she was sick before passing out. A teacher asks you where she got the alcohol from.

- What would you do?
- What should you do?

SCENARIO 2

Lucy hates babysitting for her brother Luke, who is five years old. Luke loves watching TV and screams when she tells him to go to bed, which makes Lucy angry. Lucy has heard that brandy helps people sleep and is going to put it in his hot chocolate tonight. Lucy tells you her plans.

- What would you do?
- What should you do?

COPYRIGHT © VANESSA ROGERS 2012

SCENARIO 3

You work with Ben on Saturdays at the local store and have to keep covering for him, as he always has a hangover after going out on Friday nights. You don't think it is fair that you have to do his work. The store manager takes you to one side and asks if you know what is going on.

- What would you do?
- What should you do?

SCENARIO 4

Your mum's boyfriend keeps arriving home earlier than her, smelling of alcohol. He asks you not to tell your mum that he goes for a drink with his friends after work. Tonight he arrives home after your mum and very drunk. He promises your mum that he has never done it before.

- What would you do?
- What should you do?

COPYRIGHT © VANESSA ROGERS 2012

SCENARIO 5

Claire is getting ready to go to a party and is feeling very nervous. She decides to take a bottle of her mum's wine from the fridge and drinks most of it in her bedroom. She phones you to confess what she has done and says she feels sick and dizzy.

- What would you do?
- What should you do?

COPYRIGHT © VANESSA ROGERS 2012

A DAY IN THE LIFE...

This session can be adapted into a longer series of drama scenes or a scripted play.

Aim

This activity enables young people to explore the possible consequences of alcohol through storyboards and drama.

You will need

- Flipchart paper
- Markers

How to do it

Explain that this session is going to look at 'A day in the life of a bottle of wine...'

Divide the young people into small groups and hand each group one of the scenarios. Give out flipchart paper and markers and ask the young people to discuss and agree a story of what happens as the 'day in the life' of their bottle of wine progresses. Ideas can be recorded onto the flipchart paper in storyboard or cartoon strip form. Encourage the young people to explore all possibilities for both positive and negative outcomes.

Now, explain that each group should devise a short role-play based on their storyboards. Allow about 20 minutes for the young people to develop and rehearse their piece and then call time.

Invite each group to show their role-play, whilst the rest of the young people form an audience. As each drama ends lead a round of applause and encourage feedback. Discuss the outcomes and suggest alternative endings and ways of staying safe.

'A day in the life...' scenarios

This bottle of wine is bought by a young woman using her older sister's ID	This bottle of wine is bought at the supermarket by a mother for her under-age son to take to a house party
This bottle of wine is bought at a petrol station by an 18-year-old young man to help his 15-year-old girlfriend chill out	This bottle of wine is bought by two young women at the off-licence to drink as they get ready for a big night out
This bottle of wine is delivered free with a curry ordered by young people whose parents are away	This bottle of wine is amongst home-delivered shopping, discovered by a young man whilst babysitting with a friend

COPYRIGHT © VANESSA ROGERS 2012

EMERGENCY ROOM

The issues raised in this session could be used as the basis for a short scripted drama.

Aim

This activity explores the social and biological issues surrounding alcohol consumption, by debating the ethics of treatment in an A&E department.

You will need

- A copy of the 'Emergency Room' cards for each group of four

How to do it

Start the session by explaining that at weekends many hospitals are filled with patients presenting with alcohol-related accidents and injuries. This includes older people as well as those legally too young to drink.

'According to official figures, 800,000 people are admitted to hospital with alcohol-related complaints every year – at a cost of £3 billion' (Daily Mail 2009).[3]

Suggest that with limited resources choices have to be made about who to treat first and prioritizing patients. Read the following scenario out before dividing the young people into groups of four and handing out the 'Emergency Room' cards.

'It is two o'clock in the morning on a Friday night and you are a nurse in a busy A&E department (or Emergency Room). The majority of patients in the waiting area are there because of alcohol-related incidents. You have an hour until your shift ends and so far tonight you have been spat at, pushed, vomited on and endured lots of loud abuse. All of the patients are angry, no one wants to wait and everyone thinks that they should be seen first.'

Now, explain that on each of the 'Emergency Room' cards is a summary of a patient waiting to be seen. Point out that all of the potential patients have been drinking alcohol. Each group should discuss the cards and then rank them in the order of priority that they think the patients should be seen.

Allow up to 20 minutes for discussion and then invite each group to feed back their top priorities and give reasons why. Go on to look at those cards prioritized lower down and the reasons why.

Ask the question, 'Are some patients more deserving than others?' and discuss.

---

3   Read more on this story at: www.dailymail.co.uk/health/article-1168177/Selfishness-crippling-NHS-A-amp-E-wards-overwhelmed-drunkenness-mindless-violence-teenage-pregnancy.html.

'Emergency Room' cards

A 16-year-old girl who is vomiting blood. She has been hospitalized three times already after binge-drinking vodka
A 13-year-old girl who is drunk for the first time and very emotional
A 17-year-old young man who has been arrested for fighting and being drunk and disorderly
An 18-year-old young woman who has facial cuts after being 'bottled' in a club
A 17-year-old young woman who has been found by ambulance staff drunk and passed out in the street

COPYRIGHT © VANESSA ROGERS 2012

A 19-year-old young man complaining of chest pains who has been drinking and using cocaine

A 19-year-old young man who has whiplash injuries following a drink–driving car accident

A 15-year-old girl who has been the victim of a sexual assault after passing out at a party

A 15-year-old boy who has fallen down the stairs whilst drunk and has a suspected broken ankle

A 20-year-old young man beaten up in the street after a pub fight following a football match

COPYRIGHT © VANESSA ROGERS 2012

SOAP STREET

This idea can be developed into a short play or scripted piece of work.

Aim

This role-play activity explores stereotypes about alcohol, class and gender.

You will need

- Flipchart paper and markers to record ideas
- Empty alcohol cans and bottles – a champagne bottle, a can of cheap lager or cider, an alcopop bottle, a small vodka bottle and a water bottle
- Paper or plastic bags to hide the bottles and cans in

How to do it

Start the session by asking who has ever seen a 'soap opera'. Invite the young people to call out what they watch and record it up onto the flipchart paper.

Now, facilitate a short discussion about soap operas, mentioning that most are centred around a pub, and looking at the different drinks that well-known characters drink. Ask the young people to consider what the choice of alcohol says about the character. Is there a difference in what 'educated' characters, such as doctors, drink as opposed to those without qualifications? How are characters that do not drink alcohol shown? Does this challenge or reinforce stereotypes?

Next split into groups of four, explaining that there is one 'soap style' scenario, but that each group will be given an individual card with a character on to develop. Read through the scenario twice then distribute character cards, and the appropriate prop in the bag.

Each group should now devise a short soap scene that shows what happens next. Allow about 30–40 minutes for the group to develop their plot and script.

Invite each group to perform their piece, still without disclosing what was on their character card. After each one invite the audience to guess more about the character depicted and offer feedback. Ask:

1. What stereotypes did we see?

2. What different attitudes to drinking did we see?

3. Did the wealthier characters get treated differently from the ones with less money?

'Soap Street' scenario

THE SCENARIO

Ashleigh has been taken to the local A&E department after getting drunk and passing out in the street. She was found, dazed and covered in vomit, by a stranger who called the emergency services.

She started drinking whilst getting ready and missed eating today as she didn't want to look bloated in her new dress. She has been drinking free cocktails with friends in the VIP area of a new club but got thrown out after starting a fight in the toilets.

During the night she has lost a shoe and one of her hair extensions. She doesn't remember passing out and was rude to the ambulance crew that bought her in. When she arrived at the hospital she was still clutching her last drink.

She is currently sitting in a crowded A&E department waiting for her parents to arrive.

COPYRIGHT © VANESSA ROGERS 2012

Ashleigh is 19 and the daughter of a famous ex-model and a footballer. Her social life is a whirl of parties and free promotional drinks, which she loves. She wants to be a glamour model and thinks that looks are everything so she drinks champagne, as it is lower in calories than other drinks.

Prop — Champagne bottle

Ashleigh is 18 and the only reason she got an invite to the club is because her mum is a cleaner there. Her social life is limited because she is the main carer for her grandmother whilst her mum works and she rarely touches alcohol. She would like to be a teacher but doesn't think she can afford to go to university.

Prop — Water bottle

Ashleigh is 16 and tonight she was celebrating her friend's birthday. She borrowed her elder sister's ID to get into the club, which she does most weekends. Her motto is that 'life is for living' so she doesn't have too many plans, except more parties, for the future.

Prop — Alcopop bottle

COPYRIGHT © VANESSA ROGERS 2012

Ashleigh is 17 and works in a large store. She picked up a flyer that offered free entrance to the club and got into the VIP area when the bouncer wasn't looking. She is hoping that by hanging around where wealthy men socialize she might bag herself a rich partner. To pluck up courage she gets drunk fast.

Prop – Vodka bottle

Ashleigh is 17 and is unemployed since getting sacked for laziness in her last job. She lives with her parents, but they are threatening to chuck her out as she refuses to help around the house. She tends to sleep all day and then go out with a big group of girls in the evening who are known to the police as troublemakers.

Prop – Lager or cider can

COPYRIGHT © VANESSA ROGERS 2012

REVIEW TIPS

TRUE/FALSE REVIEW

Aim

This is a really quick review to help you check out and reinforce learning and identify additional needs.

You will need

- Nothing

How to do it

Explain to the young people that you are going to call out some 'facts' about alcohol, some of which are true and some of which are not.

Participants should move to different points in the room to indicate if they think it is 'true' or 'false'. Ask the young people to keep a note of how many answers they get right.

After each round, invite people to explain their choices and to share any other related information they have before giving the correct answer.

After the last statement invite people to share their scores and note any areas that need additional work.

TRUE OR FALSE?

1. A unit of alcohol is the equivalent of half a pint of standard strength cider.
    TRUE

2. Drinking water sobers you up.
    FALSE – Time is the only thing to sober you up. The liver processes approximately one unit of alcohol per hour.

3. Drinking alcohol keeps you warm in cold weather.
    FALSE – Alcohol raises the pulse and blood pressure, making you feel warm, but alcohol causes the body to lose heat.

4. Drinking alcohol makes you go to the toilet more!
    TRUE – Alcohol is a diuretic and dehydrates the body.

5. If you drink when you are pregnant it is passed to your baby.
   TRUE – The alcohol passes into the mother's bloodstream, travels across the placenta and is fed to the foetus via its bloodstream.

6. Safe drinking limits are the same for men and women.
   FALSE – In the UK the recommended daily safe limit for men is three to four units and two to three for women.

THREE THINGS CIRCLE

This circle time activity can be adapted to suit the numbers in the group.

Aim

To review and reinforce learning.

You will need

- Nothing

How to do it

Invite the group to sit in a circle.

Ask each individual to choose three different 'things' from the session that they will remember and what they learned as a result to share in turn.

Ask each individual to choose one point and then to imagine a situation six months ahead when they are facing a problem and have a 'flashback' to the session.

ONE THING...

This is another quick and easy circle time activity that encourages young people to identify areas that they would like to learn more about and will help inform your session planning.

Aim

To enable young people to share what they have learned and what they want to know more about.

You will need

- Flipchart paper
- Marker

How to do it

Invite the young people to form a circle and sit down. Bring the flipchart paper and pen into the circle and join the group.

Facilitate a round starting 'One thing I found out about alcohol is…' followed by 'One thing I would like to know more about is…'

As the young people share their thoughts record them onto the paper and leave on display for future sessions. They can then tick off the things on the 'Like to know more about' list as the work progresses.

WORD BOX

If you have a small group ask the young people to 'post' more than one word for consideration.

Aim

To review learning and share information.

You will need

- A cardboard box
- Paper, paint, markers, etc. to decorate the box
- Post-it notes
- Pens
- A watch or clock

How to do it

In preparation for the session cover the cardboard box and decorate it. This is now the 'word box'.

Invite the young people to sit in a circle facing each other. Make sure that there is enough space for people to move comfortably without knocking into the person sitting next to them.

Hand out a Post-it note and a pen and ask each young person to write a word on it that relates to the alcohol session you have just finished. Ask that they do not show each other what they have written.

Now introduce the 'word box' and pass it around the circle asking the young people to place their slips of paper into it. Explain that for this activity every group member will have the opportunity to speak uninterrupted for 30 seconds. Stress that the role of the rest of the group is to support the speaker by demonstrating the active listening skills that they have been working on.

Once you have collected everybody's words, shake the box and place it in the middle of the circle.

In turn, each group member should then go into the middle, select a slip of paper and speak for 30 seconds about whatever is written on it. If someone picks up their own, then they should put it back into the word box and select another.

Continue until each group member has had the opportunity to be the speaker and then stop and review the process.

REVIEW QUIZ

This can be used for either individual or group work and can be adapted to use as a game (similar to True/False) for young people who do not enjoy reading tasks.

Aim

To reinforce key facts about alcohol.

You will need

- Copies of the quiz
- Pens

How to do it

Hand each young person a copy of the quiz and a pen. Encourage the young people to think back over the work they have been doing and then tick in the 'true' or 'false' boxes.

This is a quick quiz so only allow about five minutes for everyone to complete it. Go through the answers together, reinforcing messages around safety and attitudes.

Review Quiz

		TRUE	FALSE
1.	Alcohol is a drug		
2.	Black coffee cures a hangover		
3.	A unit of beer or wine has a lower alcohol content than a unit of spirits		
4.	You need to drink to have a good time at parties		
5.	People who don't drink aren't very mature		
6.	Cider is only fizzy apple juice		
7.	People who are drunk are always having a good time		
8.	You have to drink a lot before it starts to affect you		
9.	People have died from drinking too much alcohol		
10.	Adding lemonade or water to wine or spirits reduces the amount of alcohol in the drink		

COPYRIGHT © VANESSA ROGERS 2012

REVIEW QUIZ ANSWERS

1. TRUE

   Alcohol is a mood-altering drug. It slows down the action of the brain and is called a depressant drug.

2. FALSE

   Black coffee will not cure a hangover.

3. FALSE

   Units are a way of measuring alcohol so a unit is the same no matter what drink it is in.

4. FALSE

   Having a good time depends on how you feel at the time, what you are doing and who you are with rather than what you are drinking.

5. FALSE

   It is not a sign of maturity to drink alcohol. It actually shows maturity to make a decision not to drink and stick by it.

6. FALSE

    Cider is made from fermented apples and contains alcohol. It can be fizzy or traditional 'scrumpy', which is still and comes in varying strengths.

7. FALSE

    Not everyone who is drunk is having a good time, just like everyone who isn't drunk!

8. FALSE

    Alcohol affects people differently dependent on their age, height, weight and mood. Even small amounts can really affect some people and this can vary greatly.

9. TRUE

    This can be through alcohol-related accidents as well as long-term drinking health risks such as liver damage. Additionally, drinking alcohol can cause people to lose consciousness and pass out which puts them at risk of choking on their own vomit or alcoholic poisoning.

10. FALSE

    Mixers only dilute the alcoholic drink, not decrease the amount of alcohol. However, adding soft drinks to alcohol may slow people's drinking down so that they drink less.

ADDITIONAL SUPPORT

Al-Anon Family Groups UK

Tel: 020 7403 0888 between 10am and 10pm

Al-Anon is for relatives and friends of problem drinkers. Al-Ateen is especially for teenagers who have a parent or other close relative with a drink problem. This is the UK number but there are branches in Australia, Canada and USA.

Alcohol Concern

www.alcoholconcern.org.uk

Alcohol Concern is the UK national agency on alcohol misuse.

Australian Drug Information Network

www.adin.com.au

Centers for Disease Control and Prevention

www.cdc.gov/alcohol

This American site has a large section on alcohol packed with facts, statistics and support information.

DrugScope

www.drugscope.org.uk

This is a UK site with information about alcohol and drugs.